W9-BXF-671

CW

J602 T384v

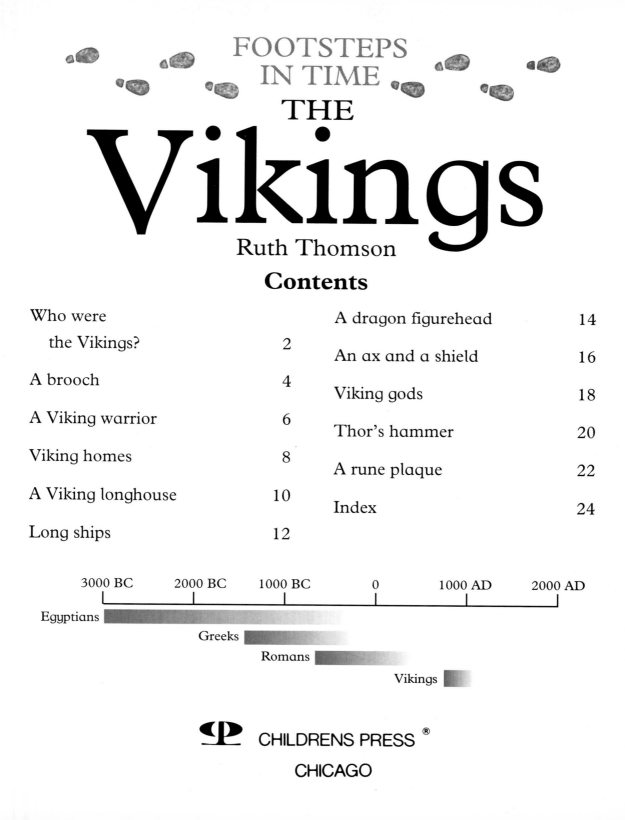

FOOTSTEPS
IN TIME

THE
Vikings

Ruth Thomson

Contents

3000 BC 2000 BC 1000 BC 0 1000 AD 2000 AD

Egyptians
Greeks
Romans
Vikings

CHILDRENS PRESS ®

CHICAGO

Who were the Vikings?

The Vikings lived over one thousand years ago. They settled around the coasts of the countries we now call Norway, Sweden, and Denmark.

There was not much good land for farming. Norway was very mountainous. Sweden was covered in thick forest. Much of Denmark was too sandy.

Greenland

Iceland

Newfoundland

Some Vikings decided to move away from their homelands. They sailed west and settled in the islands of Iceland and Greenland. Some went as far as North America.

Others went south to England and Europe. They stole treasures and took people as slaves. Some explored eastward and traded furs, honey, and weapons for silver, spices, and glass.

Norway

Finland

Sweden

Russia

Scotland

Denmark

Ireland

England

France

Spain

Italy

North Africa

Iraq

3

A brooch

Vikings wore brooches to hold their clothes in place. Women used two oval brooches. Men used one round brooch to fasten their cloaks.

You will need:

Aluminum foil   Teaspoon   Glue

Gold beads   Safety pin   Cardboard

Follow the steps . . .

1. Crumple up some aluminum foil. Press it firmly into the spoon to give it a rounded shape.

2. Glue some gold beads on your brooch.

3. Glue a circle of cardboard on the back. Tape on a safety pin.

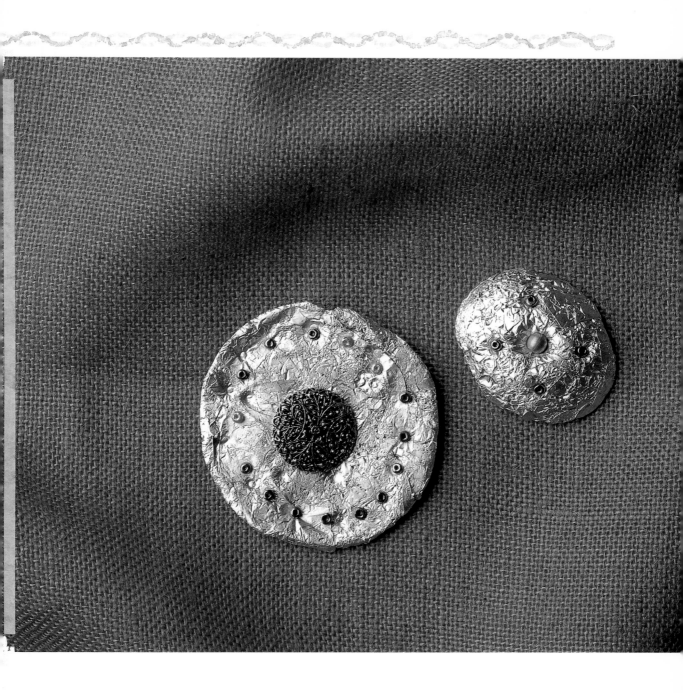

A Viking warrior

The Vikings were fearless warriors. They wore chain mail or padded tunics. Each Viking carried a sharp sword.

You will need:

Aluminum foil	Cardboard	Paints	Paintbrush
Colored paper	Pencil	Yarn	Glue
Scissors	Felt scraps		

Follow the steps . . .

1. Draw a Viking figure on the cardboard. Cut it out. Draw a face. Glue on strands of yarn for hair.

2. Cut a helmet and tunic out of aluminum foil. Glue them onto your Viking. Make a cardboard sword and shield. Add a belt made of felt.

3. Glue the Viking on some painted cardboard.

Viking homes

Viking families lived and worked in low, dark, smoky longhouses.

The walls were made of woven twigs, covered with thick mud to make them warm and waterproof.

There was very little furniture. People sat and slept on raised platforms of earth built along the walls. They kept their clothes in wooden chests. Cooking was done over an open fire. A hole in the roof let out the smoke.

A Viking longhouse

You will need:

Shoe box   Cardboard   Scissors

Paints   Paintbrush   Glue

Follow the steps . . .

1. Paint the shoe box brown.
   Paint a door at one end
   in a different color.

2. Cut a cardboard roof as long
   as the shoe box and twice as
   wide. Paint it. Fold it in half
   lengthwise. Cut a smoke hole.

3. Cut and paint two cardboard triangles
   with bases slightly wider than the shoe box.
   Cut the corners off each triangle.

4. Fold over all three edges of each triangle.
   Glue the base edge to each end of the box.

5. Glue the folded roof to the other two
   edges of the triangles.

Long ships

The Vikings built wooden ships which were light, strong, and fast. They had a big square sail, and oars for rowing down rivers. A large, heavy oar at the back was used for steering. A fierce animal head, called a figurehead, was carved at the front of the ship.

There was room for about thirty oarsmen. Each man packed his clothes and weapons into a chest and sat on it. On long journeys the men ate dried fish, hard bread, and salted meat. The Vikings had no maps or instruments. They used the sun and stars to guide them.

A dragon figurehead

You will need:

Cardboard tube   Newspaper   White glue

Adhesive tape   Paints   Paintbrush

Follow the steps . . .

1. Crumple up some newspaper. Shape it into a dragon's head. Tape it together. Push the dragon's neck into one end of the cardboard tube.

2. Mix some glue with water, and dip newspaper strips into it. Cover the head with four layers of these strips. Glue on small balls of newspaper for eyes.

3. Let the head dry for a few days.

4. Paint the head brown all over. Add eyes and swirling black patterns.

An ax and a shield

You will need:

Glue	Scissors	Cardboard
Cardboard tube	Paints	Paintbrush
Pencil	Adhesive tape	Pie pan
Corrugated cardboard		

Follow the steps . . .

An ax

1. Cut an ax head out of corrugated cardboard. Paint it gray and add a Viking design.

2. Paint a cardboard tube for the handle. Glue circles of painted cardboard over each end. Glue the ax head around the handle.

A shield

1. Cut a large circle of corrugated cardboard. Paint it. Glue a pie pan in the middle. Cut a cardboard handle. Tape it onto the back of your shield.

Viking gods

The Vikings worshipped many different gods. They believed that these gods lived in a place called Asgard, which floated above the Earth. They thought each god was in charge of a special thing, such as war or weather.

Odin, the god of war, ruled Asgard. He was fierce but wise. He was also called Woden. Wednesday is named after Woden.

Thor, the god of thunder, was big and strong. He rode across the sky in a chariot. Thursday is named after him.

Viking warriors believed that if they were killed in battle, they would go to a hall in Asgard called Valhalla. They thought that in Valhalla they would be able to fight all day and feast all night.

Frey was the god of nature.
He provided good crops and lots of sunshine.

Freyja was Frey's twin sister. She was the goddess of love, beauty, and death. Friday is named after her.

Thor's hammer

Viking men wore the symbol of Thor's hammer round their necks to protect themselves against evil spirits.

You will need:

Self-hardening clay   Ballpoint pen   Spoon
Wooden board   Cord or ribbon

Follow the steps . . .

1. Flatten some clay on a board.
   Cut out the shape of Thor's hammer.

2. Press around the edge of the
   hammer with the spoon handle
   to make a border.

3. Use the tip of the ballpoint pen to
   press a pattern in the hammer.

4. Make a hole in the top of the hammer.
   Thread the cord or ribbon through it.
   Knot the ends so you can wear it.

A rune plaque

Viking letters were called *runes*. This is their alphabet.

ᛁ ᛒ ᛌ ᛑ ᚦ ᚠ ᚡ ᚷ ᛁ ᛆ ᚴ ᛚ ᛘ ᛙ ᚭ ᛕ ᛩ ᚱ ᛌ ᛁ ᚿ ᛐ ᚠᛘᛮ
A B C D E F G H I K L M N O P Q R S T U V W X Y Z

The straight lines were easy to carve in stone.
The Vikings carved rune stones in memory of brave warriors killed in battle.

You will need:

Cardboard	Paper plate	Pencil
Paints	Paintbrush	Scissors

Follow the steps . . .

1. Trace the plate onto the cardboard. Cut out the circle you have made.

2. Paint it grey. Write the Viking alphabet around the edge. Write your name in the middle using runes.

INDEX

Entries in *italics* are activity pages

1995 Childrens Press Edition
© 1995 Watts Books, London, New York, Sydney
All rights reserved. Printed in Malaysia.
Published simultaneously in Canada.
1 2 3 4 5 R 99 98 97 96 95 94

Series Editor: Annabel Martin
Consultant: Richard Tames
Design: Mike Davis
Artwork: Cilla Eurich and Ruth Levy
Photographs: Peter Millard

Library of Congress Cataloging-in-Publication Data:

Thomson, Ruth.
    The Vikings / by Ruth Thomson; illustrated by
Cilla Eurich and Ruth Levy.
        p. cm. – (Footsteps in Time)
    ISBN 0-516-08059-8
        1. Vikings – Juvenile literature. 2. Northmen –
Juvenile literature. 3. Handicrafts–Juvenile
literature   I. Eurich, Cilla. ill.   II. Levy, Ruth, ill.
III. Title. IV. Series: Footsteps in Time(Chicago, Ill.)
    DG65.T37 1995   94-42247
    948.02–dc20   CIP
                                                      AC